21.00

JI

A LOOK AT ROCKS

FROM COAL TO KIMBERLITE

Jo S. Kittinger

A First Book
Franklin Watts
A Division of Grolier Publishing
New York ∎ London ∎ Hong Kong
∎ Sydney ∎ Danbury, Connecticut

Cover and interior design by Molly Heron
Photo credits ©: Alaska Division of Tourism: 28; Animals Animals/Earth Scenes: cover 3rd from left (G.I. Bernard), cover 4th from left, 10, 16 (E.R. Degginger), 4 (George F. Godfrey), cover left, 36, 46, (Breck P. Kent); Ben Klaffke: 53; Fundamental Photos: 35 (Richard Megna); Georgia Department of Industry, Trade & Tourism: 15 top; Helen H. Kittinger: 64; Photo Researchers: 26 (Linda Bartlett), 37 (Mark C. Burnett), 38 (Jules Butcher), 41 (John R. Foster), 39 (Sylvain Grandadam), 8 (Dale P. Hansen), 54 (Eunice Harris), 23 (Ken M. Johns), 32 (Adam Jones), 31 (Joyce Photographics), 42 (Andrew J. Martinez), 29 (Will/Deni Mcintyre), cover 2nd from left, 13 (Erich Schrempp), 45 (Art Stein), cover center (Thomas Taylor), 17; Reinhard Brucker: 22, 48, 49, 51; Scala/Art Resource: 43; South Dakota Tourism: 15 bottom; U.S.G.S. Photographic Library, Denver, CO: 24 (E.H. Bailey), 21 (HVD), 19 (R.E. Wilcox); Visuals Unlimited: 12, 30, 33 (A.J. Copley), cover right (Ken Lucas), 7 (Glenn M. Oliver).

Library of Congress Cataloging-in-Publication Data

    Kittinger, Jo S.
    A look at rocks : from coal to kimberlite / by Jo S. Kittinger.
        p. cm. — (A First book)
    Includes bibliographical references and index.
        Summary: Describes the formation and appearance of rocks, changes
        they can undergo, and how to start a collection.
    ISBN 0–531–20310–7 (lib. bdg.)   0-531-15887-X (pbk.)
        1. Rocks—Juvenile literature. [1. Rocks] I. Title. II. Series.
    QE432.2.K55 1997
    552—dc21   97-6727
                                          CIP
                                          AC

CONTENTS

We expect to see changes in living things such as this old maple. Rocks, though they may seem permanent, also change.

ONE

EVERYTHING'S CHANGING

Look around. You can see plants sprout from seeds. They grow and die. Likewise, animals are being born, growing up, and dying. You expect to see changes in the living things around you. However, when you pick up a *rock*, you might think that it, and all rocks, have remained the same since the beginning of the world. This is not the case. New rocks are continually being formed. Other rocks are undergoing change.

It is true that you can place a rock on a shelf in your room when you are five years old, and it will probably look the same when you're fifty. Unlike living things, most rocks do not change from within themselves. They change because of outside forces. If a friend comes into your room and hits the rock with a sledgehammer, your rock will break into a lot of little rocks and dust.

Forces in nature, such as wind, water, gases, heat, and pressure, are responsible for the physical and chemical changes in rocks. These forces may affect rocks either on the surface of the earth or underground.

Rocks are natural solid materials that make up the earth. What geologists call rock may seem strange to you. You leave your footprints in rock when you walk on wet sand at the beach. The clay you squished between your fingers in art class was rock, too. Rocks are composed primarily of *minerals*. As the letters of the alphabet combine in various ways to fill a dictionary with words, minerals combine in countless ways to form a planet full of rocks. All rocks can be placed into one of three broad categories: *igneous*, *sedimentary* and, *metamorphic*.

Igneous means "made by fire." These rocks form when hot melted rock, or *magma*, cools. Igneous rocks can form above or below ground.

Sedimentary rocks form from sediment. Sediment is made up of pieces of rock, shell, sand, mud, or organic matter that have been transported from one place to another by a force such as wind, water, ice, or simply gravity. When the movement stops, these particles settle layer upon layer. Sedimentary rock forms when these layers harden, or *lithify*.

Metamorphic rocks form when igneous and sedimentary rocks are exposed to great heat and pressure.

You leave your footprints in rock when you walk on sand.

**Most rocks change from external forces,
such as these pounding waves.**

Each type of igneous or sedimentary rock will change into a particular type of metamorphic rock if it is subjected to a certain amount of heat and pressure.

Because of the wide range of mineral combinations and the changes that can occur, it can be difficult to classify some rocks. *Petrologists* are scientists who describe and classify rocks. They look at several properties to determine which group a rock belongs in. The primary characteristics of rocks that petrologists examine in order to classify them are composition and texture.

Composition refers to the types of minerals that make up a rock and how much of each mineral is present. Texture refers to the size, shape, and arrangement of minerals in a rock. Some rocks have the same mineral composition but have very different textures.

This new lava will eventually cool and add another layer of igneous rock to the flank of this volcano.

TWO

FORMED BY FIRE

A VOLCANO rumbles. The earth quakes. Fiery hot magma waits beneath the surface of the earth. The pressure builds. With a roar the volcano erupts. Once magma comes out of the earth it is called *lava*. With gases and ashes, lava is thrown into the air and flows over the sides of the volcano.

As magma cools, igneous rock is formed. Where and how fast it cools as well as its mineral composition are the major factors that determine which type of igneous rock magma becomes. There are two main types of igneous rocks: *intrusive* and *extrusive*.

intrusive Rock

Not all magma reaches the surface of the earth before it cools. Sometimes magma, escaping from hotter depths, intrudes or pushes between other rocks underground. If it solidifies in these underground crevices, it becomes intrusive igneous rock. Close to the surface, magma can cool quickly, but at greater depths where the earth is hotter, the cooling takes place slowly and under more weight from the ground above. When magma cools slowly, some of the minerals inside have time to crystallize. Eventually the magma hardens into rock. The individual masses of igneous rock are called

This intrusion of igneous rock formed when magma flowed into a crevice and cooled.

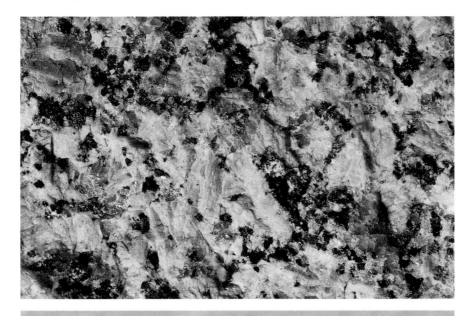

The mixture of mineral crystals in this granite give it a mottled appearance.

intrusions. Granite, syenite, gabbro, and kimberlite are four examples of intrusive igneous rocks.

Granite is a very abundant intrusive rock. Granite is formed from magma that cools slowly. As it cools, mineral crystals of feldspar, quartz, and mica have time to grow. Granite is a coarse-grained rock. If you look closely, you can see the speckles and sparkles of various minerals within the rock. Granite can be white, gray, pink, or red but is generally mottled because of the mixture of minerals.

Granite has formed very large intrusions hundreds of miles across. These huge intrusions are called *batholiths* if they become exposed on the surface of the earth. The two largest sculptures in the United States of America have been carved on granite mountains.

Stone Mountain, near Atlanta, Georgia, is one of the largest granite formations in existence. In 1923, sculptor Gutzon Borglum began a carving of General Robert E. Lee, Thomas "Stonewall" Jackson, and Confederate President Jefferson Davis on the north face of the mountain. The colossal figures are as tall as a nine-story building. Borglum left the sculpture uncompleted after an argument with those financing the project. Fifty-seven years after it was begun, the sculpture was completed by Walter K. Hancock in 1970.

Gutzon Borglum went on to become famous by creating the 60-foot-high (18-meter-high) sculptured figures on Mount Rushmore in South Dakota. The heads of U.S. presidents Washington, Jefferson, Lincoln, and Theodore Roosevelt were carved into the granite cliffs. The rocks were shaped by blasting sections away with dynamite. Before the job was finished, more than 450,000 tons of Mount Rushmore granite had been blown away.

Syenite, another intrusive igneous rock, looks similar to granite but is not a common rock. Syenite occurs in pastel colors of pink, white, gray, green, beige, and violet. It has a medium-grained texture. Granite and syenite

Gutzon Borglum carved huge sculptures into two massive batholiths: Stone Mountain and Mount Rushmore.

can both be polished and used for buildings, but syenite is used less often because of its scarcity. However, larvikite, a syenite found near Larvik, Norway, is used often for decorative facing in buildings. The arrangement and color of the large feldspar crystals in the syenite produce a blue metallic sheen when it is polished and a play of light called the *Schiller Effect*.

Gabbro is another intrusive rock frequently used in buildings. Like granite, gabbro is quite common and mottled in appearance, though it is usually much darker. Some gabbro has a blue or green sheen, much like syenite. Gabbro is also an important source of metals such as nickel and platinum.

Kimberlite is an intrusive igneous rock that forms as rare "pipes" coming up through the

Larvikite is used frequently for decorative building facings.

ground. It can be blue, green, or black depending on the proportion of minerals present in the rock. You would have a good reason to get excited if you found a kimberlite pipe in your yard. Diamonds form in kimberlite pipes. Kimberlite originates very deep in the earth, about 93 miles (150 km) underground, where the pressure and heat is great enough to form diamonds. You can visit Crater of Diamonds State Park in Arkansas and sift through the plowed-up, decomposing kimberlite. If you find a diamond, it's yours to keep. The most famous diamond mines are in Africa, where they mine the stones out of the "blue ground," referring to the blue color of the kimberlite.

A diamond in kimberlite

it forms volcanoes with gently sloping sides and can quickly flow over a large area. Rhyolitic magma erupts explosively, releasing a blast of lava and gas. Rhyolitic magma doesn't flow very easily, so it tends to form volcanoes with steep sides. The explosive eruptions can propel some rhyolitic magma far from the volcano. As each type of magma cools, extrusive igneous rocks form. Three examples of extrusive igneous rocks are obsidian, pumice, and basalt.

Obsidian is a volcanic glass formed when lava is thrown into the air. It can form from basaltic or rhyolitic magma. It is generally black but can be gray or streaked with reddish-brown. It cools and hardens so rapidly that crystals don't have time to grow, thus it becomes a smooth, dark glass. Obsidian occasionally forms as long filaments called "Pele's hair." These clumps of golden brown strands look like glassy wire. Pele is the legendary Hawaiian goddess of volcanic fire.

Another legend associated with obsidian concerns Apache Tears. Rounded pieces of obsidian can be found scattered in the western United States. According to Apache tradition, the *nodules*, called Apache Tears, mark the spot where an American Indian died. Sometimes, people tumble angular pieces of obsidian into smooth pieces and then try to sell them as genuine Apache Tears.

Primitive people used obsidian to make arrowheads and tools. When obsidian is chipped, it breaks off in rounded pieces called *conchoidal fractures*. This

Pele's hair

allows it to be formed into points with sharp edges. By examining objects made of obsidian found at ancient Indian sites, archeologists can figure out how long ago people lived there.

This dating is possible because of a method called *obsidian hydration*, which was first recognized in 1960. When a fresh surface of obsidian is exposed to the air, water in the air begins to slowly diffuse, or move, from the surface into the center of the rock. By examining an obsidian object under a microscope, archeologists can

tell how long this process has been taking place and therefore determine how long ago the obsidian was exposed to the air. They can then determine how long ago the object was made. By using this method to date an obsidian projectile, American Indian presence in Yellowstone State Park has been traced back at least eleven thousand years.

Have you ever seen a rock float? Pumice can. Pumice is an extrusive igneous rock formed primarily from explosive rhyolitic eruptions. When a gas-filled mass of lava is spewed into the air, the gas bubbles expand and the frothy

This obsidian blade was made hundreds of years ago. Notice the rounded depressions on the edge of the blade. Because obsidian breaks along these conchoidal fractures, it is easy to craft sharp edges.

Because pumice is filled with so many air bubbles, it is light enough for this man to easily lift two pumice boulders. In fact, it is light enough to float in water.

lava cools and hardens into pumice. This rock, which is usually light colored, looks like frozen foam. In fact, the name pumice comes from a Latin word meaning foam.

Basalt is a type of rock that forms when basaltic lava flows out of a volcano. It forms the cone of the volcano and covers the surrounding land. Basalt, like obsidian, is generally black. However, over time it can change to

Basalt, formed from cooling lava, can accumulate to incredible thicknesses.

brown or red when iron in the basalt oxidizes. *Oxidation* occurs when a substance chemically combines with oxygen. A form of oxidation that you're probably familiar with is rust, which forms on iron metal.

Basalt is by far the most widespread extrusive igneous rock. After repeated eruptions and lava flows, basalt can accumulate to incredible thicknesses of many thousands of feet and can cover thousands of square miles. In fact, a layer of basalt lies beneath all the ocean floors, which make up two-thirds of the earth's surface.

Such massive beds of cooled lava are called *flood basalts*. The buildup of basalt from underwater volcanoes can also create island chains, such as the Hawaiian islands.

When a thick basalt flow cools, it sometimes breaks into six-sided columns. Two incredible examples of basalt columns are found in Fingal's Cave in Scotland and The Giants Causeway in nearby Northern Ireland.

Fingal's Cave is on Staffa island, a 75-acre (30-hectare) island of caves belonging to Scotland. It is the only known cave in the world formed of basalt columns. The sea flows into the cave and over thousands of years has carved a huge cavern. The massive *hexagonal* columns of basalt create the feeling of a giant vaulted hall. The famous composer, Mendelssohn, was inspired to write an overture entitled "Fingal's Cave" or "The Hebrides" after a visit to the cave in 1829.

The Giant's Causeway, in Ireland, is another expanse of large basalt columns packed tightly together. The tops of the columns form stepping stones that lead from the foot of a cliff and disappear into the sea. One legend has it that an Irish giant named Finn MacCool fell in love with a lady giant on the island of Staffa. Supposedly he built the wide highway of columns across the sea from Ireland to Scotland to bring her to his home.

Another tale says that a Scottish giant, Bennendonner, built the causeway from Staffa to Ireland. His plan was to invade Ireland. In this story, Finn MacCool dressed up like a baby to scare Bennendonner away.

The Giant's Causeway

When the invading giant saw the huge baby he fled back to Staffa, wondering how big the parents of a baby that large must be. He destroyed the rock bridge as he went, but remnants of the highway remain on both ends.

THREE

THAT SETTLES iT

JUST AS A brick mason builds a wall by adding one row of bricks on top of another, the earth builds sedimentary rocks layer by layer. Sedimentary rocks are created in four stages: *erosion, transportation, deposition*, and *diagenesis*.

Rocks exposed to water and air are constantly being changed by weathering and erosion. Rain, wind, and ice wear away small pieces of stone. Earthquakes, floods, glaciers, and people with bulldozers and dynamite remove more.

Transportation is the movement of these pieces of rock, mud, and sand. Wind sweeps sand away. Glaciers plow rocks in their path. Particles are washed into low-lying areas and into streams by rain. As the rock fragments are tumbled about, the bumping

Glaciers grind up existing rock and transport the fragments a long way. When the sediment is finally deposited, it may solidify into sedimentary rock.

grinds the edges smooth. You can see rounded pebbles and rocks when you wade in a creek. Your feet stir up the silt and sediment on the bottom. There can be a long path of transportation from the site of the original rock. For example, rock eroded from the Grand Canyon in Arizona can be carried down the Colorado River to the Gulf of California about 400 miles (644 km) away. Eventually, some of the material goes all the way to the ocean.

Deposition is the laying down of the material when it finally stops moving. One layer after another is deposited in the same place. The weight of the overlying layers presses out water and squeezes the material together. Minerals in the water, such as silica, carbonates, and iron oxides, then cement the particles into rock. This process is called diagenesis.

Sedimentary rocks are not formed only from rock fragments. Shells, minerals or organic matter can also build up in layers. Over time they can become rock as well. There are three main categories of sedimentary rocks: clastic, chemically formed, and organically formed.

Clastic Rocks

Clastic is the largest group of sedimentary rocks. The name comes from the Greek word *clast*, which means "fragment." Clastic rocks are those formed from deposits of pebbles, rock fragments, sand, or clay.

The silt-laden Colorado River contrasts with the clearer waters of the Little Colorado River. Some of this sediment will travel all the way to the Gulf of California before it comes to rest.

A conglomerate sedimentary rock consists of distinct rounded pebbles.

The size of the clasts or particles in the rock is important in classifying these stones. Puddingstone is a common name given to a *conglomerate* sedimentary rock that has distinct rounded pebbles, suspended like cherries in Jell-O. A conglomerate is a mass of different objects stuck together. The finer material between the larger fragments is called the *matrix*. The smoothness of the particles in puddingstone indicates that the small rocks were tumbled in water before they settled and cemented into a conglomerate.

The fragments that make up breccia have rough edges.

If you find a piece of sedimentary rock with rough, sharp chunks of smaller rock cemented together, it is *breccia*. You can tell by the sharp edges that the particles did not travel far before being deposited. They may have been fragments caught up in a mudslide that raced down a mountain.

Sandstone, you can guess, is made of grains of sand cemented together. Sandstone feels gritty when you rub it. Its color and strength depend on the material that cements it together. Sandstone may be yellow, brown, red, gray, or green. The presence of iron oxide gives a rusty hue. Cobalt, nickel, and titanium result in richer colors. Silica provides the strongest cement.

These ancient sand dunes
have hardened into sand-
stone. The patterns made
by the once swirling sands
are captured in the rock.

Shale has the smallest particles of all sedimentary rocks. Shale is made from clay or mud. The particles are so small that no additional minerals are needed to cement them together. The material simply binds together when under pressure. Shale is generally gray but can be pink, red, black, brown, buff, or green. Some pieces of shale have captured patterns of raindrops or waves from some vanished sea.

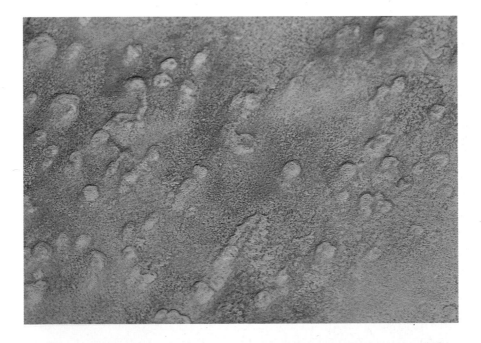

This piece of shale preserves the imprints of prehistoric raindrops.

Chemically Formed Rocks

Chemically formed sedimentary rocks form when minerals dissolved in water are deposited over time. One way this occurs is when rainwater percolates through the ground. For example, if water seeps through limestone in the ground, the water will dissolve the mineral calcite (which is made of calcium carbonate) from the limestone. As the water evaporates in cracks and caves, the dissolved calcite is left behind. Stalactites and stalagmites are examples of chemically formed rocks that form in this manner.

Stalactites form as water drips from the ceiling of a cave. Stalagmites form when the water drops hit the floor. In both places, traces of calcium carbonate are left behind. Eventually they build up, or down, as the case may be. Carlsbad Caverns in New Mexico contains some of the world's largest and most spectacular formations of chemically formed sedimentary rocks. You may have visited there, or gone *spelunking* to see stalactites and stalagmites in another cave.

Chalcedony is another rock that can form as a chemical deposit. Its name is derived from the ancient city of Chalcedon, a Greek city in Asia Minor. Varieties of this rock are used as gems and in jewelry. For example, bloodstone is a birthstone for March, agate for May, and carnelian or sardonyx for August. All of these are types of chalcedony.

Agate is the banded variety of chalcedony. It forms in

The stalactites and stalagmites of Carlsbad Canyons are examples of chemically formed sedimentary rock.

hollows containing dissolved quartz in water. As the water evaporates, layer after layer of agate grows within the hollow. Round balls filled with agate are called *geodes*. Sometimes they are completely filled with agate. Often they are hollow with several layers of agate and

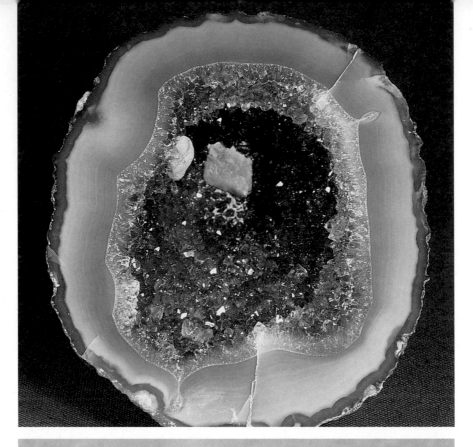

This geode is lined with bands of agate and quartz crystals.

crystals in the center. Occasionally you can shake a geode and hear some water still inside.

Organically Formed Rocks

The third category of sedimentary rock is formed from organic deposits. These are deposits of previously living things. Shells, skeletons, and vegetable matter can change into stone under the right conditions.

Fossiliferous limestone is made of clearly visible shells, coral, and ammonites. However, in compact limestone, the particles of shells and fragments of microscopic animals are so small they cannot be visibly identified. Limestone can originate beneath a body of fresh water or the ocean. One way to test for limestone is to pour vinegar on the rock. Most limestone will bubble when exposed to vinegar. The famous white cliffs of Dover in England are made of limestone. At some points, the chalky cliffs stand more than 300 feet (91 m) high above the sea.

Coal is proof that a rock can be made out of plants. Ancient swamps created tons of plant matter. The plants grew, died, and then sank to the bottom. This formed thick layers of *peat* in the swamp. Over the years, the peat was buried under sand or other material. As with other sedimentary rocks, the

This limestone reveals the fossil of an ancient coral.

increasing weight of additional layers provided the necessary pressure to turn the peat into coal.

Coal is a black or brown rock that has the unusual ability to burn. The energy of the plants, stored in the stone, becomes the fuel for the fire. Because coal was developed from living matter and can burn, it is called a fossil fuel.

Plant material still accumulates, year after year, in places such as the Everglades swamp in Florida. Eventually, new coal may form from the plants that are dying today. To think that a watery swamp plant can change into a burning rock is incredible.

Coal has the unusual ability to burn.

Sedimentary rocks of various types often accumulate in layers on top of one another. These layers are called *strata*. The Colorado river has cut through layers of sedimentary rock to create the Grand Canyon in Arizona. Visitors can view layers of limestone, sandstone, and shale of all colors. But you don't have to go to Arizona. Look for stratification where highways have been cut into mountains. If you find a safe place to explore sedimentary rocks, look closely. Plants and animals trapped between layers can be preserved as fossils.

Each layer of rock is like an entry in a diary that whispers secrets to those who read the earth. Geologists can see which animals and plants lived in each era. They can see when volcanoes erupted and fires blazed. Sedimentary rock fascinates scientists and rock hounds alike.

The Grand Canyon features layers upon layers of sedimentary rock.

FOUR

CHANGiNG TiMES

Just as a butterfly goes through metamorphosis, changing from a caterpillar into a butterfly, rocks can also be changed over time. *Meta* means change and *morph* means form. Metamorphic rocks are completely changed in structure and appearance from the original rock.

Heat and pressure are the two basic instruments of change. High temperatures can be caused by nearby magma, hot gases, or simply the intense heat deep within the earth. Pressure results from the weight of the earth above or from the movement of plates within the earth's crust. These high temperatures and intense pressure deep within the earth can cause physical and chemical changes to occur in rocks. In addition to changing the existing texture and mineral composition of the rock, sometimes new *elements* are introduced by hot liquids and gases that flow within the earth. The new metamorphic rock can differ in color, *hardness*, and texture from the original rock, called the *protolith*.

Most change occurs over long periods of time. However, a cataclysmic event, such as the impact of a meteorite, can also produce extremely high temperatures and pressure. In such cases, surrounding rocks can be changed almost instantly. This type of *metamorphism* is called shock metamorphism. An impact can be so powerful that it can form tiny diamonds. Another example occurs when lightning strikes sand. The sand can fuse together into a metamorphic rock called fulgurite.

A lightning strike has fused sand particles into this piece of fulgurite. This instant change is called shock metamorphism.

Slate is a metamorphic rock that forms from shale.

Each type of igneous or sedimentary rock will change into a particular type of metamorphic rock. For example, shale turns into slate. Peridotite turns into serpentinite. Limestone changes to marble.

Slate is a metamorphic rock that splits easily into flat pieces. It is usually gray but can be black, brown, green, red, or purple. Schoolroom blackboards were once made of slate. Today slate is used as flagstone to pave patios and sidewalks and is sometimes used on roofs of houses.

Serpentinite is generally green with a veined appearance. If you see a rough piece of serpentinite, notice the *luster*. It looks dull or waxy. Touch it. It feels smooth and somewhat greasy. Serpentinite has been used since ancient times for jewelry and art objects. It is soft enough to carve, and it polishes well. In the stone and trade industries, serpentinite is often called just serpentine, like the mineral. It is also mistakenly labeled as green marble at times.

Serpentinite has been used for art objects since ancient times.

True marble started out as limestone. Under heat and pressure, the calcite within the limestone recrystallizes and forms large, coarse grains of calcite. This process is called recrystallization. A rough, broken piece of white marble will look like a lump of sugar.

Pure marble is white, but other colors are common when impurities such as clay minerals are present. The colors can be solid or have a veined effect when the impurities are swirled throughout the rock. Colors can include buff, yellow, pink, red, green, gray, and black.

Many types of marble are used in beautiful buildings around the world. However, pure white marble is the most prized. Famous sculptors, including Michelangelo, have chosen white marble for its beauty and reliability. It will not split when carved, and it polishes to a silky smoothness. Statuary marble also has a special luster that comes from the rock's *translucence*. Light penetrates the marble a short distance and reflects off the crystal surfaces inside.

The Lincoln Memorial in Washington, D.C., is made of white marble. It holds a huge seated figure of President Abraham Lincoln created by sculptor Daniel Chester French. It remains one of the most inspirational and beautiful monuments in the capital city.

Marble is mined in quarries around the world. Georgia, Nevada, and New York have important marble resources in the United States. Marble does not split easily and may shatter if explosives are used. Therefore, spe-

The Lincoln Memorial is made of marble, a metamorphic rock that forms from limestone.

Mica schist

cial mining equipment is used to carefully cut the rock into large blocks.

Metamorphic rocks present a real challenge to petrologists who classify rocks. The degree of change from rock to rock can vary tremendously, and a metamorphic rock can undergo further change and become yet another rock. Simple metamorphism changes shale into slate. But if the pressure that formed the slate continues, mica crystals in the rock can grow larger. The slate has then changed to phyllite. This is a fine-grained rock that glitters with microscopic flecks of mica. If the pressure continues even longer, the mica crystals grow still larger. The phyllite then becomes mica schist.

FIVE

ROCK HOUND ROUNDUP

PEOPLE COLLECT all sorts of things—baseball cards, coins, stamps, Happy Meal toys. Why do people enjoy collecting? Collections can show the history of a sport or country. Sometimes people make lots of money when collectibles increase in value. But most people collect things just because they like them.

The same things can be true of a rock collection. The history of our planet as it has changed is recorded in its rocks. Some rocks increase in value. But most rock hounds just love rocks.

The wonderful thing about rock collecting is you can start wherever you are. Rocks are all around you. Simple tools are all you need. A good hammer and a book to help you identify rocks will get you started.

A prospector's pick

A special hammer, called a prospector's pick, is helpful when working in hard rock. It acts as both a hammer and a pick. As your hobby develops, you may add shovels, chisels, probes, screens, a magnifying glass, and a gold pan to your stock.

Always get permission when rock hunting on other people's land. Unprotected rocks will scratch and break one another, so take some newspaper along on your rock trips to wrap your best specimens. But be sure not to litter or damage property.

When you find new rocks for your collection, be sure to make a note of when and where you found them. You'll want this information to make a permanent label when you get home. Your best samples of each type of rock can be organized into a nice display.

First wash your rocks carefully to remove dirt. Toothpicks, toothbrushes, and dental picks help remove dirt from crevices. Other rock hounds can give you tips on how to clean stubborn stains on various rocks.

The most organized collectors make up a catalog and numbering system for their rocks. A number is placed on each rock. Then information about that rock is put in a notebook next to the corresponding number. You can devise a system in which all similar rocks start with the same prefix, such as S for sedimentary, etc. In the note-

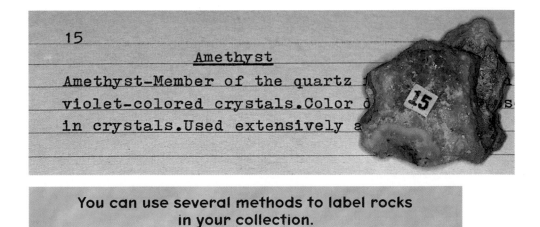

You can use several methods to label rocks in your collection.

book, record what type of rock it is, if you know, and the place and date it was found. The numbers can be placed on the rocks in a few ways. You can cut a tiny rectangle of heavy paper and write a number on it with waterproof ink. This is then glued to the back of a rock. Or you can paint a small white rectangle on the back and write the number on the paint when it dries. Alternatively, you can paint a small rectangle with whiteout, write the number on the whiteout, and then coat the label with clear nail polish for protection.

Place your rocks in separate shallow boxes such as jewelry gift boxes. These can then be grouped in larger shallow boxes, such as the ones cases of soda come in. Eventually, you may want to find some special shelves or a case with drawers to keep your collection in. With all the changes that have occurred in the earth's crust, well-kept rock collections have been very useful to geologists who study how the rocks from an area have changed in the recent past.

Beyond cleaning, some rock hounds take further steps to beautify their rocks. You may have noticed the brilliant colors of rocks in a stream. When the rocks dry, however, their colors seem to fade. The "wet" look can be captured by polishing rocks. A rock *tumbler* is used to accomplish this process. Rocks are placed inside the tumbler's barrel along with a rough grit. The grit grinds off the edges of the rocks as it tumbles around and around. In the first stages, a rock tumbler brings about

A rock tumbler has smoothed these rocks and given them the "wet" look.

some of the same changes a river does as it tosses and tumbles rocks. The grit is replaced in the tumbler every week or two with progressively smaller particles. Finally, during the last week, a polish is added to the rocks. When finished, the rocks are smooth and shiny. The tumbling process will only work on hard rocks. Soft stones will break or crumble in the tumbler. Vibrating machines are available that will smooth stones in about half the time of a tumbler, and other machines will polish flat surfaces of rocks.

Agencies, organizations, and clubs around the world are gold mines of information about rocks. The United States government has Geological Survey offices in every state. Geologists at the United States Geological Survey (USGS) are helpful and friendly, ready to answer all your questions. You can even ask your questions by way of the Internet! Most Geological Survey offices also sell maps, books, and reports about geological subjects. Canada and many other countries have similar offices, and most states have local state survey offices.

The American Federation of Mineralogical Societies is made up of local rock and mineral clubs around the country. In addition to field trips, workshops, and educational talks, these clubs offer the combined knowledge of all their members. Rock swaps, auctions, and shows are often sponsored by these groups. Clubs are open to people of all ages. Many old-timers like nothing better than teaching new members about the rocks they love. Call your local chamber of commerce to see if there is a club in your town.

With a little effort you can find other sources of information. Try searching for "rock hound" on the Internet. Newsletters and magazines on rocks can be ordered,

Members of rock and mineral clubs are usually eager to share their knowledge.

bringing information as close as your mailbox. Ask if there is a natural history museum in your area. They often include geological exhibits. And if you are ever in Washington, D.C., be sure to visit the Smithsonian's National Museum of Natural History. The American Museum of Natural History in New York also has an extensive rock collection. Just be sure to wear comfortable walking shoes! Another place to check out is the earth science departments of nearby universities. They sometimes have rock exhibits or clubs as well.

The crust of our planet shifts and changes constantly. Rocks change as a result. The next time you are out collecting, pick up a rock. Close your eyes. Imagine what it might have gone through. Is it an igneous rock? Did it explode out of a volcano, or was it hot magma that found a place to escape the heat within the earth. Is it sedimentary rock? Is it made of fragments from a high mountain top, washed down and carried by rivers to the sea? Is it a metamorphic rock? Was it squeezed so hard it had to change from the inside out? Rocks hold many mysterious secrets, yet at the same time, they provide many clues to the history of our planet.

Your local college or university may have a rock and mineral collection. This is Harvard University's display.

Glossary

batholith   a huge mass of intrusive igneous rock that has been exposed by weathering.

breccia   sedimentary rock made of rough, sharp chunks of smaller rock cemented together.

clasts   fragments of rock within sedimentary rock; these fragments were once part of other rocks and can be as small as grains of sand or as large as boulders.

conchoidal fracture   smooth, concave, shell-like patterns formed when some rocks, especially glasses, are broken.

conglomerate   rock made of rounded rock fragments or pebbles cemented together in a matrix.

crust   the uppermost layer, or rocky skin, of the earth.

deposition   a laying or putting down.

diagenesis   the physical and chemical changes that occur as sediment changes into sedimentary rock.

element   one of the pure substances that make up all matter. An element cannot be broken down into a simpler substance.

erosion   the process of wind and water wearing away soil and rock.

eruption   the bursting forth of lava from a volcano.

extrusive   rock formed from lava that has extruded, or been forced out, onto the surface of the earth.

flood basalt   immense beds of solidified basaltic lava.

geode   a rounded rock mass, originally hollow and usually lined with agate and crystals.

hardness   the measurement of how easily a mineral is scratched.

hexagonal   having six sides.

igneous rock   any rock formed from magma as it cools and hardens.

intrusion   a mass of igneous rock formed beneath the surface of the earth.

intrusive   rock formed when magma works its way between rocks and hardens beneath the surface of the earth.

lava   melted rock that pours out onto the surface of the earth from a volcano.

lithify   to change from layers of sediment into rock.

luster   the shine or "look" of a mineral depending on how it reflects light.

magma   melted rock beneath the surface of the earth.

matrix   the finer material between the pebbles or rock fragments of a conglomerate or breccia.

metamorphic rock   rock created when igneous or sedimentary rock is changed by heat and pressure.

metamorphism   a change brought about in a rock from heat and pressure.

mineral   a naturally occurring substance with a specific chemical composition and a crystalline structure.

nodule   a rounded lump of rock that separates easily from the surrounding rock.

peat   partly decayed plant matter found in ancient swamps that can be used as fuel.

petrologist   a scientist who studies and classifies rocks.

protolith   the original rock from which a metamorphic rock is formed

obsidian hydration   a method used to determine the age of obsidian by the amount of water contained within the sample.

oxidation   changes that occur when some materials are exposed to oxygen.

rock   natural solid material that makes up the earth's crust, usually consisting of a mixture of minerals.

Schiller Effect   a reflection from some minerals that is almost metallic, sometimes bronzy.

sedimentary rock   rock formed from many layers of sand, mud, rock fragments, and/or plant or animal remains that have undergone pressure from the ground or sea above.

spelunking   exploring caves.

strata   layers of rock; the singular form is stratum.

translucence   letting some light pass through but not enough to see objects clearly on the other side.

transportation   the carrying of sediment from one place to another by rain, wind, water, and other natural forces.

tumbler   a machine with containers, or barrels, that tumble around and around to smooth and polish rocks placed inside.

weathering   the breakdown (but not transportation) of rocks on the earth's surface by natural forces such as rain, ice, and wind.

Organizations and information

Organizations
U. S. Geological Survey (USGS)
Eastern Region and National Headquarters
USGS National Center
507 National Center
12201 Sunrise Valley Drive
Reston, Virginia 22092
1-800-USA-MAPS
http://www.usgs.gov/
Ask-A-Geologist E-Mail: Ask-A-Geologist@usgs.gov

Central Region
U.S. Geological Survey
Box 25046 Denver Fed. Ctr.
Denver, Colorado 80225

Western Region
U.S. Geological Survey
345 Middlefield Road
Menlo Park, California 94025

Magazines

Earth
21027 Crossroads Circle
Waukesha, Wisconsin 53187

Rock and Gem
4880 Market Street
Ventura, California 93003

internet Resources

Bob's Rock Shop *http://www.rockhounds.com/*
This noncommercial site features a gallery of images, which
now features over 150 specimens. The site also provides numerous articles on rock and mineral collecting as well as an
extensive list of links to other rock-related sites.

Geologylink *http://www.geologylink.com/*
This site offers fascinating geological information geared to-
ward students, teachers, and enthusiasts. They feature several sections dedicated to kids.

The Mineral Gallery *http://mineral.galleries.com/*
The Mineral Gallery is an online rock and mineral shop.
Their site offers lots of information on rocks and minerals
including photos of specimens for sale.

Rockhounds Information Page
http://www.rahul.net/infodyn/rockhounds/
This site includes a list of answers to questions frequently
asked by rockhounds. They also feature a library of images,
articles, and links to many other sites.

For Further Reading

Bains, Rae. *Rocks and Minerals*. Mahwah, New Jersey: Troll Associates, 1985.

Fuller, Sue. *Rocks and Minerals*. New York: Dorling Kindersley, 1995.

Holden, Martin. *The Encyclopedia of Gemstones and Minerals*. New York: Facts on File, 1991.

Krafft, Maurice. *Volcanoes: Fire From the Earth*. New York: Harry N. Abrams, 1993.

Lauber, Patricia. *Volcano: The Eruption and Healing of Mount St. Helens*. New York: Bradbury Press, 1986.

McConnell, Anita. *The World Beneath Us*. New York: Facts On File, 1985.

Schumann, Walter. *Handbook of Rocks, Minerals, and Gemstones*. Boston: Houghton Mifflin, 1993.

Silver, Donald M. Earth: *The Ever-Changing Planet*. New York: Random House, 1989.

index

Italicized page numbers indicate illustrations.

About the Author

Jo S. Kittinger finds creativity in nature. As a potter, freelance crafts designer, writer, and illustrator, she can take common clay and turn it into a vase, or a summer's breeze and turn it into a story. Her work has appeared in numerous books, magazines, and newspapers. She is the author of Watts First Book *Dead Log Alive!* She lives with her family and a menagerie of pets in Hoover, Alabama.